Gail Ashton

If this was a map
of your life

Indigo Dreams Publishing

First Edition: If this was a map of your life
First published in Great Britain in 2024 by:
Indigo Dreams Publishing
24, Forest Houses
Cookworthy Moor
Halwill
Beaworthy
Devon
EX21 5UU

www.indigodreamspublishing.com

Gail Ashton has asserted her right under the Copyright,
Designs and Patents Act 1988 to be identified as the author of
this work.
© Gail Ashton

ISBN 978-1-912876-84-6

British Library Cataloguing in Publication Data. A CIP record
for this book can be obtained from the British Library.

Designed and typeset in Palatino Linotype by Indigo Dreams.
Cover art by Ronnie Goodyer from his original photo.
Printed and bound in Great Britain by 4edge Ltd.

Papers used by Indigo Dreams are recyclable products made
from wood grown in sustainable forests following the guidance
of the Forest Stewardship Council.

For aunty June
(22/06/41 to 16/06/19)

and for Michelle and Nettie, always

If we take eternity to mean not infinite temporal duration but timelessness, then eternal life belongs to those who live in the present
~ Wittgenstein

Acknowledgements

Enormous thanks to my dear friends Jenny Cooke and Sue Tyson for comments on early drafts; not forgetting Will Kemp; or Nettie and Michelle. Any infelicities remain solely mine.

Thanks to Dawn and Ronnie at Indigo Dreams for all their support and for jointly awarding me the Geoff Stevens Memorial Prize for Poetry 2023.

Some of these poems, or versions of them, were first published in *Obsessed with Pipework, Sarasvati,* and *The Dawntreader.*

A version of 'What if we were to ask the fire?' was first published in *The Other Side of Glass* (Cinnamon Press, 2012).
An earlier version of 'All this' appeared in *From Hallows to Harvest* ed. Adam Craig (Cinnamon Press, 2019).
Versions of 'When', 'indoors for much of the winter', and 'I love this time' appeared in *in the voice of trees,* eds. Jan Fortune & Adam Craig (Cinnamon Press, 2020).
'Should I walk to her old house again and give you the story of her shopping bag?' was shortlisted for the Indigo Dreams Autumn Poetry Prize 2023.
'Once all this was fields' riffs on the title of Robert MacFarlane's book *Is A River Alive?* – forthcoming 2025.

CONTENTS

If this was a map of your life

This comes from a place of interruption

What if it was mid-
August – it is –
and the magnolia's

> aflame, two crimson
> candles kindling the corner
> of our garden

> > and hawthorn already
> > yielding its berries
> > seasons out-

> kiltered but still
> enough. Remember
> this as you pass,

glass in hand,
the moment gone
in a slur of blue.

> This time is
> extraordinary,
> as are you.

Would you read this story in my hands?
for Sue

I can talk to you of anything, this
woodpecker at a window, fiction,
should the peculiar frettings of

the mind ever let us go? So open
this email, take whisky to consider
air drifting with ease. Answer these:

shall we dance without punctuation
through origami leaves? Could birds
spark jubilation, this uprising of trees?

You find these things to be true

almost a day spent
in the garden cutting
back Black Lace, buddleia,

seedheads of sedum,
carmine buds miracles
of forgetting and you think

on all the different ways
time catches us out,
your late aunt husked

on a hospital bed saying
*I never thought it would
come to this* or your father

at a gate passing
in or out, the latch
a clink against wood,

those years of never
speaking until he writes
I've done the garden

and it looks good, this
robin a bright garnet
bead of attentiveness.

What is more possible than this moment?

Day has worn us down
but still you keep this
garden at your back

        when you are reading
        and on the other side
        of our French doors

                the house is a violet
                brimful of lemon-
                scented bright.

What we salvaged from the woods
for Nettie

Here you are again
the gift of air passing
beneath the moss of over-
                hanging trees.

You are water
fall of silvered light
supple   willow
woman in the shape
of possibility and though

                you are stepping
                away from me
                I would touch
                your shoulder   say

                    you are something
                    more than this
                    cloud of startle   leaf.

If we could live each day like this
for Irene

Euston to New Street you talk the entire journey,

       face a daisy inflected in a streaming train-glass,

       then, after years of interruption, in the garden
       centre at Ashbourne, you greet me

       mid-

conversation, hair petalled at the rim of your hat.

       And did I never tell you the sheer joy of that?

As summer slips its hand from mine

I'm thinking on journeys
I've never made,
nor wish to,
how the thirteenth moon
blooms, an orange

        lantern, not blue at all,
        on the Italian
        for lover – *amante* –
        and my mother's
        locket, *te amo* it said,

inscribed on her birthday
card which arrived
each year, no matter
where we moved,
save that summer, four

        days short of forty-one.
        I had yet to come home.
        They say a bear can become
        a bird, earth could swallow
        sea. But no-one told me

how to carry these things.
Until I heard the ring
of weather on the breeze
and far-off murmurs
from this stand of trees.

Note: lines 18-19 from words by Kathleen Jamie, *Surfacing*

Our forgotten hearts

He sits on the hill where once a windmill
opened its arms to sun, his loose-leaved shirt
an orange sail on a southern breeze, fields

all bronzed and stubble. And you look straight through
his *will you lie with me a while* to the whole
planet whirring above, the tick of earth

below. He follows you home but you have
no interest in boys like him. Just the warmth
of skin and summer brushing off the light.

Woven from wonder & hope

"Courage is what love looks like when tested by the simple everyday necessities of being alive."
~ David Whyte, *Consolations: The Solace, Nourishment and Meaning of Everyday Words.*

Somewhere in the night your heart
migrates to a shoulder, sleep-
carried to a place you cannot
know while water in a blue bowl
draws an anatomy of our space
for love.
                    Small marvel this,

how light hardens into stone,
days open with what takes you
to the window, *my cherie amour* drifting up the stairs, voices in woods
and *everybody's free to feel good*,
one minute catastrophe, the next
Nettie on a wall, a girl again, teasing
sky apart with her piano fingers.

How to fall into white
for Michelle

So, evening is bleaching
out and your wine glass

tipped with rosé trembles
on the table you're wiping

with a cloth of clouds
and your face opens a door

into a room beyond
as it did when time slipped

a blue-white gown over
the first of your treatments

and how I wish I'd wished
you this light singing light

in its small bones, the larks
this morning's thousand possibilities.

Knowing what this moment needs of me

Your mind is on distant views,
mine here, where hare's
curated in grass, its amber

rhythms abbreviated by shadow.
Should I follow the open plains
of its feet we would fly through

upland snow to when you
and I no longer meet.
This hare is liquid bone-

rivered light from the neck
of a jar. Something tells me
we will never travel that far.

Why aren't my friends in this garden?
for Jenny

Where would I put you if you came?
Perhaps in the shade near the weather
vane and the lemon-candled magnolia.

> Or have you under a parasol eating
> ice-cream again each of us taking
> turns to read aloud. Between the lines

of these swallow-dipped borders bees
fall into the faces of flowers and afternoon
blossoms tea in our Japanese pagoda.

> I will prune the apple to a singing
> bowl of sky. Think of you in northern
> hills waiting on spring to roll in with

oh there you are, what took you so long?

What if we were to ask the fire?
for Pat

Awake most nights, you take your
watercolours into the small hours,
lose the way wherever you go.
Once we met in library stacks, now

beneath the damson, pockets full
of dog treats, wondering how
the Riverside Chaucer came to be
in the laundry basket. You say,

your house is full of tables, hope
they don't turn on you. Next
you have a story about a journey.
Love Pat, at nearly bedtime.

You will never know your voice
is full of sherbet lemons.

.

Once all this was fields

October's here early my love, all snap and witch-
bone light. Soon night will be dribbling down
windowpanes and at the gate deer shiver
like water. You will recall it. Except for owls

and rasp of fox, this is the quietest of times.
I have been searching the box, you know the one,
it's in the attic next to the broken phone.
Nothing I write is what I intended to say. But

these days I too am a much quieter woman.
What's happened is done, and despite all
you might have heard I still wait for
the kingfisher on the lips of our bridge.

Should you ever come, I would ask is a river alive,
a tree, a bird? Ours was a discourse of roses,
words with thorn at the heart. I tend them faithfully
though we are but a single mountain ridge apart.

What would it look like, this letter to myself?

Tethered to home I wander
from room to room
shocked by purple and gold
spiking the garden, a last flush
of roses alight in a tawny acer.
I could gather apples
from Sheila's orchard, wind-
fall of an early winter
at my back, wonder
how we arrived at this
house still not quite ours

though the ghost has
long gone and everywhere
new and pale and airy,
the foal at the gate soft
beneath my hands. Horses
have worn a path through
the paddock, the last
of the phlox an inheld
breath should we grace it
with our presence, lift
our skirts, and ride it.

After sunset has lowered itself into the hill

> Oak emails her thoughts wondering
> why I wear a skin so pale.

She says roots are wings for
inverted clouds and bark knows more

> than it's prepared to say. Her mind
> is full of half-formed things.

The old ways. Abandoned
babies wormed into the breach.

> The creaking of her ancient heart.
> How birdsong pulls winds apart.

When

they felled the oak
down the lane

birds stopped singing
and ours shed her last

winter leaves in shock.
At night her breathing

slowed. I heard her
heartwood knock knock

against the glass
of stars. And even now

she wears the call
of owls not knowing

how to be still
ever fill the space

The forest has a tongue

I am
ash oak thorn.
For every new-born
plant one tree.

Say ilex salix.
Repeat after me. Sallow.
Willow slows the flood.

A culture is no better than its woods.

I am
larch-tongued juniper
betula pendula quercus quercus
malus sorbus.

Leave us
our language of longevity.

Leave me faerie
Avalon gospel gibbet.

I am
river-worn. Drawn
from memory purity medicine
your lungs your lights.

I am
rock-a-bye-baby.
Yew for chemo
therapy sacred.
Tree of life.

I am
greenleaf translated
into runes.

I married a tree and the tree married me.

I am ruin.
Your long-ago. The future.
Deathblow.

When the tree falls, how can the shadow stand?

I have a soul you know.

Note: quotations taken from WH Auden ('A culture is no better than its woods') and Mary Lavin, 'In the Middle of the Fields' ('When the tree falls, how can the shadow stand?').

I love this time

Wood reads the air, finds it wanting.
Speaks moss and birch, is raining deer.
Lives between words of hollow light,

fallen late to shape a stream. Knows
those things that do not linger.
Carries a place we thought was winter.

Children are living in the trees

West wind a cradle, leaves
a girdle for sleeping forms.

Newborns tucked in cleft of
tree dream wild garlic, dogs

violet, dogs mercury. Cloaked
in lichen, hollow, fern they learn

the anatomy of winter mother.
That ash won't splinter, hazel

will bind. You will not find them,
bark a cover for their shame.

They cleave to root, script
unfurling from the inside out.

I don't know that

dusk folds up the day
behind it a forest full of holes

in the garden you are wearing
white-frost stars clematis still out

I am carrying a river through
rain and so much ruined light

Just tell me you're okay

Two years on I find you in the sideboard,
nothing but skittered bills and balances.

You're a wry seal on a funeral card
trying not to draw attention to yourself.

It wasn't like this when you were alive.

So what will I do with your vanishing,
here, then not, your vital signs bleached

to paper, this day I could climb into,
were it not for the shape of its mouth?

Who told me I could say it?

Say I could anchor this moment
in a morning shoring up rain or
press it into the paper of a birch.

What difference would it make
to that diagnosis? Or the fact that
this is the closest we can travel

with you now. Later we will fret
over the photograph gone from
your handbag, too late to stop family

ransacking the flat. This is the story.
I don't know whose it is. But I carry it
as long as you want. Write the letters.

Tell them you were more than our aunt.

Not so extravagant

I would go to greenwood
for there is cure in alder,
though you wouldn't know,

nor how to draw it down,
and how underfoot
never settles but shivers,

like myself, padding
a locked house, in search
of boots and hidden keys.

Come morning, I think
on all the different ways
of breathing. A kitchen

happens around me, tea,
coat to straighten a walk,
and overhead geese, brush-

strokes on parchment sky.
Look, they say, such
astonishment at a water's edge.

While you were leaving

We carry on as best
we can, make tea, pack
your things, a way
of pretending this door
doesn't open onto a day
we have never seen, that

        at the last your hand's
        grasp so sudden, strong,
        and this thrush won't spill
        its throat of forgotten notes,
        and in case you think
        this easeful, we won't.

        Someone tries to
        empty the bin while
        you lie here, dead,
        and we sit on, silent,
        waiting to learn how
        we might ever begin.

We are the gatherers

How dark already, holly-laden,
berries almost stripped
from every hedgerow.

Lanterns stutter in moth-soft
borders, a night from once ago
when brothers, neighbours,

furred with snow, abandon
woods and hidden valley.
Winter kicks at heels, the tracks

ahead a light-starved path.
What if they left and never
came back? On days like these

we bar the doors, draw close
to fireside's spit, every window
lit, still calling someone home.

This is how we used to be

"Equindo uscimmo, a riveder le stele..." ~ Dante
And so we come forth, and once again behold the stars

I would have us sleep
under trees, know dialects
of moor and grass, feel
pulsing rivers run
tributes beneath our feet.

That we are drifting a

                                             part

is the least of what we say.
So maybe now
is not the time to tell
you behold this field of stars.

We cannot walk this coast without her

Mad for marram grass
and spray she's spanned

> our leap through gorse
> and sea. Now she waits

> in a spill of dunes
> ears tuned east

> as if – like me – to see
> who might rise through

salt and hail us.
It's the last we say

> every year each of us
> older north tilting

> closer her head still
> ebony on my knee

> horizons stretched tight
> and everything here

so bright   set
so fiercely bright.

Should I walk to our old house again and give you the story of her shopping bag?
for my mother (28th July 1939 to 24th July 1979)

This Velux window is open
eye and I am sleepless, thinking
on the poet who kept a skull

> called Moses in a Viennese cake
> box, what kind of gift is that,
> its every angle worn by

the grind of words on a cliff's
page-edge and I'm wondering
how will I cross the early draft

> of that street tomorrow, the one
> that passes our house, it used to be
> a meadow, we could have washed

our hearts in it, only now there's no-
where to put this grief, save
the bedroom, it's still there,

> a wardrobe at its margins, exactly
> where hers used to be and today
> I would have her again in fields

wringing out the light, saying
me bloody shoes are all wet, her face,
water-marked at this window,

> on the sill three books,
> a box of eclairs, radio
> blaring in the kitchen below.

All tomorrow

I'm at a piano translating snow-
fall into song, afternoon still lit by
a moon courting the candelabra

of a winter tree. And I'm reminded
how each day paints itself from memory,
our holly so thick with scarlet berries

I could touch them and never wear out
their velvet. I dream of walking through
barley with you and our dog, coming

home to plant astilbe or listen for
the barking of the fox in the wood.
But I know the unlikelihood of that.

For now your hands are on the barrow
and beside us this - the throat of a
sonata falling me down the steps

of sleep. Your voice saying *all tomorrow
untouched my love* and on a slope of sky
the Milky Way unlocks her heart to dawn.

On this day, your brother's funeral
for Geoff

Also my birthday, the card you sent,
interesting, and the dreams in which

       you abandon me, repeatedly.
       I'd almost forgotten but there you both are,

       identical shovels slumped on a step,
       your brother's braces, his *what took you*

              so long? And the sudden blow
              of camassia simmering in the yard.

All this

          forgetting
the bud of flame in
          your rowan
          famine moon
strewn at its feet
          the house

every flared eye fastened to
          ribbons
of snow and below
wind-rushed fields
          nail tongues
of lark to willow

You would love that
for Karen

And if I spoke to you of agrimony,
Good King Henry, coltsfoot called
stargazies. Or sent you smellfox,

fairy flax, alkanet, you would laugh
and dig another bed for the stripping
of rabbits. And we'd say, *ey up missus,*

and *what's t'do*, and read of cherry plum
planted in a north corner against the dark
while all around you rivers flex

these hills and rain turns your spade
to dripping ink and you are filled
with skylark, so many tumbling words.

As if the day's pattern has gone with the tide

I had thought to find you in woods
though you never go. But still I waited

on the fallen log where that September
I found a bag of weed in early leaf fall,

solace of a different kind. Then
last night came on its own

terms and frosted the same old path
to the crook of our lane. And there,

your face, hoar-smoke above a hedge,
and arms linked we step the road,

each astounded footfall all we lost,
all we still might want to know.

This winter's day falls to cinders
for Sue

We came late to these afternoons,
tentative with tea, fingers tuned
to horizons only absent
words might reach.

The hare on the fireplace speaks
in bronze and we wait on its grace,
stillness like leaf-fall gathered
in our dusk-drawn hands.

indoors for much of the winter

emptying the dregs
of evening into a bowl

stars at a window wanting
to come in and you are

a vision with your life
of torn petticoats

hands a skeleton of ash
trees pointing up night

I will tell you this for nothing (During Covid)

"Our memory is outside us, in a rainy breath of time."
~ Annie Ernaux, *The Years.*

Hours become days become
weeks with us trying
Qi Gong, baking, our books.

Pat's vaccination story,
her *shoot me when*
it comes to this and

all the time sparrows
embroiled in a hedge.
Some of us grow

older, unnoticed. Do not
be afraid though stars are
loosening in the jawbone

of dawn and frozen fists
of damsons sit in a dish.
Sometimes you remember

it anyway. Time a vast
grass ocean shaking
splinters from sea-birds'

glassy wings. Memory outside
us, its breath the last thing
we thought we'd heard.

Well, we'll just have to see

She can't abide a dry dinner, will go
to twenty and not a penny more.
Well, nobody told me anything about it,
 she says, wishes it would rain.

We plan her birthday. She thought
she'd done with all that, skin marked
like braille. When she's moved to
a side room, all the women fall silent.

Water, she says, the cannula in
her hand emptying into sodden
sheets again. Three in the morning,
and the doctor can't explain why

he won't examine her. *Protocol,*
he says. *We'll see on Monday.*
His bleeper is a bird fluttering
away down a treeless corridor.

Looking for a door to the woods

"For me the door to the woods is the door to the temple..."
~ Mary Oliver

Today rain came, with it a scent
of leaves and ashen light.

I have a small rowan. Its delicate
greens rinse the corner of a yard.

I would speak to the woody shade
of our cypress. We are to sit,

it says. Wait out this quietude.
There will be leverets in the field

below and we will be singing
Que sera sera in the hope that,

sound really is the last sense to
go and at your passing the open

throat of a morning thrush drenches
the sill with cherry blossom.

Nothing is as emerald as the snowdrop's hidden eye

And in this way, I am reminded how
your voice steps out from under trees to say

there is remedy for all things should we
but open our mouths to this fragrant light.

If this was a map of your life

You might shape it in communion
with rain, for what else is there in this place,
bar thorn bush, spindle, which take us

   the long way home. And would you mark
   this house, its lighted windows startled
   in your eyes, the colour of moors, smoke-

      screen for hawthorn, fleabane, teasel.
      Here birdsong thrilling in our ears
      and yet you follow this wet afternoon

   along the contours of a ripening sky,
   trees breathing in time with the lift
   of your boots, myself at a table, waiting.

Indigo Dreams Publishing Ltd
24, Forest Houses
Cookworthy Moor
Halwill
Beaworthy
Devon
EX21 5UU
www.indigodreamspublishing.com